ENGLAND'S WORST FOOTBALLERS

ENGLAND'S
WORST
FOOTBALLERS

JEFF STELLING

WEIDENFELD & NICOLSON

CONTENTS

INTRODUCTION

So what do I mean by 'the worst'? For the purpose of this book, it's those footballers who have proved the worst value; those with the worst goalscoring record; those with the worst disciplinary records. It's the players who were unfit or uncommitted. Or both. It's those who were unlucky. And those who will for ever be remembered by their club's fans – but not usually for the right reasons. Sometimes a single own goal (or in Frank Sinclair's case half a dozen of them) or solitary missed open goal (sorry, Gordon) has been enough for a player to be condemned throughout his career by the more critical supporters.

The players included here were nominated mainly by fans, fan clubs, ex-players and managers past and present – nothing whatsoever to do with me, you understand! You may not agree with all of them – in fact, I'm sure you won't – and I hope you will argue your worst-ever over a pint or two.

Everyone included in these pages has one thing in common. They are all better players than me! In fact, if there had been a page or two on Sunday morning football, I could easily have qualified thanks to an unfortunate capacity to put the ball past my own keeper whenever a chance, or half chance, came along. Right foot, left foot, head, knee or bottom, I could despatch them in every possible manner. I could also qualify in any contest to find worst golfers, cricketers, tennis or squash players.

And I have already been warned by one ex-pro – who doesn't feature in this volume – that he is planning a book on the worst TV presenters ever…

Jeff
Stelling

THE PREMIERSHIP

The crème de la crème…

…that sometimes turn sour

ARSENAL

JOHN JENSEN

Some players have an eye for goal. For others it's a blind spot. When John Jensen signed for Arsenal, memories of his brilliant goal for Denmark in their famous victory over Germany in the European Championship final of 1992 were still fresh in the minds of Gunners' fans. When he left four seasons later, they would have just one more to remember. Jensen was never prolific for his country – just four goals in total. But his failure in front of goal for Arsenal made him a cult figure. He did finally break the drought in a 3–1 defeat at Queens Park Rangers. The commemorative 'I was there when Jensen scored' could at last be worn. Unlike London buses, one did not follow another for Jensen. When he left the club in 1996 to return to Denmark on a free transfer he had scored just once in 138 appearances.

In Ian Wright's first 138 games for the Gunners he scored just 106 more than the Dane.

Ironically it was the transfers of Jensen and Norwegian Pal Lydersen that would eventually bring about the downfall of one of the club's finest ever managers, George Graham. The Arsenal board sacked him after deciding that he hadn't acted in the best interests of the club when signing them.

Jensen is prominent in most 'worst player' polls at Arsenal, though he was often rivalled by a player who scored even less goals. In 50 appearances Gus Caesar failed to find the net and was often the butt of ridicule at Highbury. He was swiftly freed by Cambridge United, Bristol City and Airdrie before finally joining Colchester United. There, ten years after joining the staff at Highbury, Gus finally scored his first English league goal.

JOHN JENSEN

11

ASTON VILLA

BOSKO BALABAN

Aston Villa paid £5.8 million of Doug Ellis's precious cash to bring Croatian striker Bosko Balaban to England in 2001. Two years later he could still walk the streets of Birmingham totally unrecognised. Not surprising really as he hadn't started a Premiership match. He had managed just eight substitute appearances and had failed to score a single goal.

It had all looked so hopeful. Balaban had scored 14 goals in 27 games for Dinamo Zagreb and had been the top scorer in the Croatian League for two successive seasons. He was an established international with half a dozen goals for his country. Former Villa striker Alan McInally dubbed him a future superstar and manager John Gregory called him an exceptional talent who was ready immediately to take his place in the Villa attack. Sadly, he wasn't and never would be.

His only starts came in a Uefa Cup first round tie a month after he had been signed and a Worthington Cup game against Sheffield Wednesday two months later. Even then he was substituted after an hour.

Later Gregory admitted, 'The truth is he never looked like scoring – not even in training. The boys called him Savo – after Savo Milosevic, another less-than-prolific striker.'

Balaban said, 'It was a nightmare two years. I signed for five years and I have spent two years in the stand.'

Villa eventually loaned him back to Zagreb. But even then they paid a large portion of his £20,000 a week wage. By the time Villa terminated his contract in December 2003, he had become the most expensive mistake in the club's history.

BIRMINGHAM CITY

ALBERTO TARANTINI

Argentinian players were all the rage after their World Cup final victory over Holland in Buenos Aries in 1978. It was a terrific team with the likes of Mario Kempes, Ossie Ardiles and Daniel Passarella.

Alberto Cesar Tarantini played in all of the home nation's games and even though he was a full-back scored a crucial goal when they met South American rivals Peru.

While Ardiles and his compatriot Ricky Villa would be resounding successes at Tottenham, Tarantini would be a resounding flop at Birmingham City.

City manager Jim Smith paid a club record fee of £295,000 to take Tarantini to St Andrews in November 1978. What Tarantini had was a furious Latin-American temper. What he lacked was any discipline or positional sense. He never looked happy and lasted only 23 games in the Midlands – but they were eventful games.

When Manchester United's Brian Greenhoff was mysteriously laid flat out after an off-the-ball incident, the Argentinian was asked for his opinion on what had happened. His comment, 'I think he's just tired' hardly helped to defuse the situation.

His brief sojourn in England ended in typical Tarantini style. Offended by heckling, he waded into his club's own fans at St Andrews for a punch-up – 17 years later Eric Cantona would famously try to do the same thing at Selhurst Park.

It's not the last time Birmingham City have had their fingers burnt by signing an Argentinian. In July 2003, they paid £2.5 million to Rosario Central for their top scorer Luciano Figueroa. The young striker was given a free transfer before Christmas – just seven months into a five-year contract. He had played only three minutes of Premiership football...

BLACKBURN ROVERS

EGIL OSTENSTAD

Blackburn Rovers' fans were relieved when Kevin Davies returned to Southampton after his traumatic stay at Ewood Park. He had cost the club more than £7 million – but by the time he left two seasons later he had scored only one league goal.

As part of his move back to the south coast, Norwegian international striker Egil Ostenstad joined Rovers.

Ostenstad had done well at Southampton – never more so than when scoring a hat-trick in their 6–3 win over Manchester United at the Dell. But his career then took a downward turn from which it would never recover.

The problem for Ostenstad was that although he would often start a game and sometimes finish one, the two would rarely happen in the same match.

Astonishingly in 81 appearances for Rovers, he only completed the full 90 minutes eleven times. His stop-start stay yielded just 13 goals.

It was the same story when he had the chance to go on loan to Manchester City. He started only one game – but inevitably failed to finish it – and came on as a substitute in three others.

Not surprisingly when he was eventually allowed to join Rangers, coaching staff found him to be ring-rusty. He failed to score at all in the SPL before being released at the end of the season.

Ostenstad isn't the only striker to find it hard to score for Blackburn. Since Alan Shearer's 31 league goals in 1996, no Rovers' player has managed even 20 goals in a top-flight season. The most spectacular recent failure is of course Corrado Grabbi, whose £6.75 million move from Ternana yielded just 5 goals before he was mercifully allowed to return home to Italy.

BOLTON WANDERERS

BARRY FRY

It was just Barry Fry's bad luck to be a winger at Manchester United in 1963. It was the year that another winger arrived at Old Trafford, and Barry would be the first to admit he was no George Best. Best would go on to play 361 games for United and score 137 times. Fry never made the United side and twelve months later would be told he had no future at Old Trafford. Fry made the short trip to Burnden Park, then the home of Bolton Wanderers.

There he got his chance in the first team and the footballing world saw the famous Fry celebratory gallop when he scored his first ever league goal in a game against Cardiff. Gordon Taylor, these days the Footballers' Union boss, but then a winger, crossed the ball. Wyn Davies, leading the home attack and gentle giant John Charles, at the heart of the visitors' defence, both missed it leaving Fry to head home. Not only was it his first league goal. It was his last. After three games, he was given a free by Bolton. He joined Luton but after six games was again freed. In two spells at Leyton Orient he managed another seven starts. Both ended the same way – with a free transfer.

Barry reckons he would have done exactly the same thing had he been any of his managers. It would be enough to dampen the enthusiasm of many a man, but not Barry Fry who has gone on to become one of the game's most colourful managers and biggest characters.

CHARLTON ATHLETIC

CARL LEABURN

There have been few more honest, harder triers in the game than Carl Leaburn. And few consistently less prolific.

In 14 years of league action, the strapping Lewisham born striker scored a grand total of 57 goals – harshly put, that's four a year.

Leaburn could lead the line, hold the ball up, win it in the air, but he couldn't put it in the net. Or at least not often.

It didn't look as if it would turn out that way when he scored for Charlton Athletic as a teenager soon after making his debut in 1987. It was his only goal that season. Or the next. In the 1988–89 season, he did manage to score twice in his 32 appearances. But any hopes that this would open the floodgates were soon dashed. He failed to score the following season. And managed just one goal the next. If you are losing count, that's a total of four goals in his first five seasons.

By now Leaburn's goalscoring feats were legendary. But suddenly he discovered the Midas touch in front of goal and scored no less than 11 times in the 1991–92 season. It was his best ever campaign.

In January 1998 Wimbledon paid £200,000 for big Carl. Three goals in his first four games made that look good value. Unfortunately he managed only one more in his next 55 appearances. The Dons' manager Terry Burton gave him a free transfer in May 2001.

A third London club, Queens Park Rangers, took on Leaburn. But he made only one appearance as a substitute for them. And no, Carl didn't score.

CHELSEA

WINSTON BOGARDE

A player's career can stall due to bad luck. In the case of Winston Bogarde it could be put down to bad timing.

The Dutch international had enjoyed a glittering career with Ajax, where he had won a European Cup winners medal, AC Milan and Barcelona. He had played in the 1996 European Championships and the World Cup two years later.

He described his move to Chelsea on a Bosman in 2000 as his ultimate dream. He wasn't to know that within two weeks the man who signed him, Gianluca Vialli, was to lose his job. Vialli had apparently chosen him ahead of Aston Villa and England defender Gareth Southgate.

New boss Claudio Ranieri took a look at him and decided he didn't like what he had seen. After four appearances the Dutchman was consigned to the reserves. But Bogarde had signed a four-year deal at more than £40,000 a week. He decided he wasn't going anywhere. The outcome was that he became the biggest outcast in British football and a hate figure at Stamford Bridge.

Bogarde didn't play again in the first team after an appearance in the League Cup at Gillingham in November 2002. At the start of the 2003–4 season, he wasn't even allocated a shirt number.

He claimed he never missed training – though it was always with the youth team – and said he always gave his all. No one elsewhere was prepared to take him on, so Bogarde stayed put for four years until the summer of 2004. It was an expensive impasse. Bogarde describes his decision to join Chelsea as terrible. His bank manager disagrees.

It's not only overseas players who have failed to make the expected impact at the Bridge. Robert Fleck had been top scorer for four consecutive seasons at Norwich City. In 1992 Chelsea paid more than £2.1 million for the Scot. But 40 games yielded just three goals, before he was packed off back to Carrow Road for a fraction of the original fee.

CRYSTAL PALACE

MICHELE PADOVANO

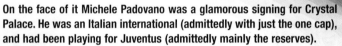

On the face of it Michele Padovano was a glamorous signing for Crystal Palace. He was an Italian international (admittedly with just the one cap), and had been playing for Juventus (admittedly mainly the reserves).

But he had shown enough to persuade Palace to pay £1.7 million for him and for former England captain Ray Wilkins to describe him as 'an asset to the Premiership'.

He was anything but an asset. In his spell at Selhurst Park he started just eight matches and never played more than two in a row. His strike in a draw with Leicester was his only goal during his stay in England.

By the time he had left on a free transfer, Palace had been relegated and Chairman Mark Goldberg bankrupted after pumping around £25 million into the club – much of it on sky-high salaries.

It wasn't the last the club heard of the Italian. When Palace went into administration, he got in touch – allegedly to claim a million pounds in unpaid wages! Perhaps he needed the money, as by now his career had plummeted and he was playing his football in Italy's Serie C.

EVERTON

BRETT ANGELL

The chance to score in the Premiership is a dream for any lower league striker. But it can turn into a nightmare.

The same sized goals can suddenly seem so much smaller.

Brett Angell had been a consistent goalscorer for both Stockport County and Southend United. In January 1994, the recently appointed Everton manager Mike Walker decided to give him his chance in the top flight.

It turned out to be a terrible mistake for both the manager and player.

At 6 feet 2 inches and 14 stone Angell was very different physically from the man he had been bought to replace, Everton legend Tony Cottee.

Their goalscoring records would be very different, too. Cottee scored close on a hundred times for the club. In fourteen troubled months, Angell would score only once. As he struggled, so did Everton. In November 1994, Walker was sacked after just 10 months – the shortest reign of any manager in Goodison Park history.

Angell lasted little longer. In March, Everton accepted a £600,000 bid from Sunderland manager Mick Buxton.

In a fanzine poll at the end of that season, 72 per cent of fans voted Angell the player they were most pleased to see leave.

His agony didn't end there. In a year-and-a-half he failed to score a single goal for the Wearsiders before returning to Stockport.

Back at the club where he had made his league debut, Angell rediscovered the scoring touch that had so cruelly deserted him and scored 78 times for the club at a rate of almost one every other game. By the time his career ended he had played for 14 different league clubs.

After quitting the game he became a shelf stacker at Tesco. But showing the resilience that helped him overcome his Merseyside misery, he would later become a sports management consultant and football pundit.

FULHAM

PETER BAAH

French international striker Steve Marlet cost Fulham more than £11 million when he was signed by Jean Tigana from Lyon in 2001. He turned out to be so poor – with just 10 goals in two seasons – that the club tried to avoid paying the full amount, refusing to pay the final instalment until FIFA ruled that they must.

But fans who believe he was the worst player ever to wear the shirt have short memories.

In the early 90s the club that now graces the Premiership was battling for survival in the bottom half of the football league. Instead of Edwin van der Saar, Sean Davies, Steed Malbranque and Luis Boa Morte, the tiny crowds at Craven Cottage were watching Jim Stannard, Duncan Jupp, Udo Onwere, Martin Pike and Gary Brazil. And Peter Baah.

Baah joined Fulham in 1992 after making just one appearance for his home-town club Blackburn Rovers. He says his debut for Rovers was the biggest thrill in his career.

Supporters at Fulham were less thrilled with their new signing who frequently crops up in debates over their worst performers. 'He had no redeeming features' claimed one cruelly, 'not even a good anecdote'. In two seasons in West London, he managed just four goals in his 49 appearances under Don McKay and Ian Branfoot.

By the end of the second season, Fulham had been relegated to division three and Baah had played for the final time.

After a brief spell at non-league Northwich Victoria, Baah headed for the United States – and nine years on was still playing for Indiana Blast.

LIVERPOOL

SEAN DUNDEE

There are plenty of recent contenders to be Liverpool's worst-ever player. They paid £3 million to Auxerre for French international Bernard Diomede, who made just four full appearances. That was four more than Jean Michel Ferri who was already 32 when he joined the club for £1.7 million from Turkish side Istanbulspor. Frode Kippe who cost £700,000 from Lillestrom was with Liverpool for two-and-a-half years before making his first-team debut. His big moment came against Grimsby in the Worthington Cup when he came on as a substitute. It probably didn't help his Anfield career that Liverpool lost that night.

They were all Gerard Houllier signings – but the Frenchman bore no responsibility for signing the player who fans regard as unquestionably the worst to wear the red of Liverpool.

Roy Evans' search for a striker to provide competition for Michael Owen and Robbie Fowler took him to Europe where he paid £2 million for Karlsruhe's South African born striker Sean Dundee. This seemed a little surprising at the time as the German side had just been relegated to the second division. Dundee's failure to score – he managed just three goals all season – was one of the main reasons they'd gone down.

On Dundee's arrival in England he told supporters that he was as fast as Owen, but he wasn't.

After coming off the bench twice early in the season, he failed to even make the bench for the next six months. He did get three more chances as a substitute later in the season, but couldn't manage a goal.

Liverpool cut their losses and packed him off to VfB Stuttgart where he proved his failings in front of goal were no flash-in-the-pan, scoring just 24 goals in his next four seasons in the Bundesliga.

MANCHESTER CITY

CHRISTIAN NEGOUAI

When Christian Negouai joined Manchester City in November 2001, manager Kevin Keegan told the club's official website that the player could be anything he wanted to be. What he turned out to be was trouble.

In his home debut following his £1.5 million move from Belgian club Charleroi, the giant Martinique born midfielder was called a cheat by Rotherham manager Ronnie Moore after punching the ball into the net for an equaliser. In his very next game against Blackburn he was red carded after less than half an hour and has failed to command a first-team place since.

He then infuriated Keegan by ignoring the club's medical advice and going abroad for treatment to an injury. The treatment went badly wrong and left him needing operations on both legs!

He missed all the following season while recovering. He was also fined £2,000 for missing an FA drugs test, claiming he had misunderstood that he needed to provide a sample due to language difficulties.

By the start of the 2003–4 season the Frenchman was finally fit – and started for City's reserves only to be sent off for lashing out at a Sunderland player.

He did get a chance in City's first team later that month when he played – and scored – in the Uefa Cup qualifying round second leg against Total Network Solutions. But it wasn't to kickstart his career in England. He failed to play for the first team again during the season.

After almost three years, Negouai, the player who could be anything he wanted to be, had started just two league matches, one in the League Cup and one in the Uefa Cup.

Even Keegan had run out of patience. 'He has done some silly things and made some poor decisions' he said.

MANCHESTER UNITED

MASSIMO TAIBI

Old Trafford is known as the 'Theatre of Dreams' but some remember it more for the personal nightmares they endured there.

A move to the world's biggest club must be impossible to resist. But even players with an outstanding pedigree have found it hard to live up to expectations at Manchester United. England international striker Gary Birtles had already won two European Cup winners medals with Nottingham Forest when he was signed by Dave Sexton in October 1980 for £1.2 million. He failed to score at all that season and would eventually wait almost a year for his first goal. Not surprisingly, he proved to be Sexton's final signing and eventually returned to Forest for a fifth of the original fee.

But it is goalkeepers that have had the greatest problems. Peter Schmeichel was so good that he's proved almost impossible to follow – just ask Massimo Taibi, who is widely regarded as the worst-ever United player.

Taibi joined United for £4.4 million from the Italian club Venezia. His stay was short and eventful. Taibi had done okay in his first couple of games – but the doubts set in with one of the most famous blunders of all time. Matthew Le Tissier's 30-yard daisycutter was barely powerful enough to reach the goal, yet somehow managed to nutmeg the hapless Italian and earn Southampton a draw at Old Trafford. The United faithful didn't know whether to laugh or cry. Things got still worse when Taibi was blamed for at least two of the goals as United crashed 5–0 at Chelsea in the first week of October.

He never played for United again.

One keeper who spent even less time on the pitch for United was Nick Culkin. He joined from York in 1995 and finally made his debut five years later when Raimond van der Gouw was injured against Arsenal.

Culkin came on, took a goal kick, only for the referee to immediately blow for full time. His debut – and his United first-team career – were over after just six seconds!

Manchester United's Massimo Taibi has a particularly bad day at the office. He had to pick the ball out of his own net an astonishing five times in a home game against Chelsea in 1999.

MIDDLESBROUGH

MARCO BRANCO

Middlesbrough fans have swayed to the samba beat ever since Juninho arrived at the Riverside. In his third spell at the club, he remains a folk hero on Teesside.

Other Brazilians have been less successful. Emerson produced some fine performances too in his years there – when the club could find him that is. His disappearing acts were frequent. But his goals still ensured he was a crowd favourite.

So it was with a real sense of anticipation that Boro fans welcomed a third Brazilian to the club in February 1996. After all Branco was a World Cup winner and had 78 caps – even if he was 32 and looked a stone overweight on his arrival.

He also had a reputation for scoring wonderful free kicks.

In fact, his reputation was so good that 17,000 Boro fans turned out to see him make his debut for the reserves. The burly Brazilian did his best. He took every free kick and shot at goal every time, whether it was from 20 yards or 40 yards. He hit the floodlights and the corner flag, but never the target.

Branco managed just five first-team appearances that season – and just one the next, before Boro paid up the remaining eight months of his expensive contract. The ageing former superstar then headed to the United States for one final big payday with the New York/New Jersey Metrostars.

His time on Teesside though wasn't totally wasted. By the time Branco left he had allegedly mastered five words in the English language: pass, shoot, goal, lager and nightclub. And he was still a stone overweight.

NEWCASTLE UNITED

ELENA SIERRA MARCELINO

Older Newcastle United fans felt that former Queens Park Rangers winger Wayne Fereday – 41 appearances and no goals in the 1989–90 season – should be considered their worst-ever player. Fereday might even agree – he described his move as the worst he could have made. The supporters didn't care for him and let him know their feelings every game.

French World Cup winner Stephane Guivarc'h was another St James' Park flop as he managed only a single goal in four starts before being moved to Rangers. However, most agree the biggest disappointment in black-and-white history has been Elena Sierra Marcelino.

Ruud Gullit paid £6 million to Real Mallorca for the Spanish international in 1999. He was substituted at half-time with a groin strain during his debut for United. It was an indication of what was to follow, although his St James' Park career would be wrecked by a different injury – to his finger.

The defender snapped a tendon in his finger at Old Trafford during the opening game of his second season with Newcastle. So bad was it, that he managed only six appearances that season, bringing his total to 17.

When the club paid him off in 2003 he had still been seen only 17 times. His appearance on February 11, 2001 at Charlton had proved to be his last. Sir Bobby Robson's patience had finally run out.

In addition to the transfer fee, he had earned £3.5 million in wages as well as £500,000 to leave, which worked out at well over half-a-million pounds per game. But was he grateful? Not a bit! 'I was called a thief who was robbing the club's cash' he claimed afterwards. 'The fans preferred a clash of heads to intelligent play.' There's no question about which United players head they hoped would be involved...

NORWICH CITY

DEAN CONEY

Dean Coney had a terrific career at Fulham, where he scored more than 50 goals. His spell at Norwich was less successful. His only goal in 17 games reportedly bounced off his knee – but they all count.

A hernia problem and snapped cruciate ended Coney's Carrow Road career.

Controversial wing back Pape Diop also has claims to be the Canaries' worst-ever player.

The Senegal born player arrived on a one-year deal from Lens in August 1999. He lasted just four months and managed just two league starts. On and off the field he was unpredictable. The fans liked his turn of pace and dribbling skills, but his lack of any positional sense had coaching staff in despair.

Diops' stay ended prematurely after allegations that he spat at fans during a Boxing Day match against Queens Park Rangers at Carrow Road. Four days later he had signed for French second division club Racing Club de Paris. Manager Bruce Rioch denied he'd been packed off because of the incident, but City fans think differently.

PORTSMOUTH

YOSHIKATSU KAWAGUCHI

When you need a big, strong keeper to dominate your penalty area, Japan isn't the most obvious place to look. But Portsmouth looked there – and found Yoshikatsu Kawaguchi.

In October 2001, they paid a club record £1.1 million to Yokohama Marinos for the 27-year-old goalkeeper who was a cult figure in his homeland. His face appeared on posters, keyrings and phone cards and he was a regular on television adverts. He'd even been voted second most handsome player in the 1998 World Cup behind David Beckham, though admittedly this was in a poll run in the Hong Kong *Star*. It's fair to say that he would never be idolised at his new club.

By the time he arrived at Fratton Park, he had won 52 international caps. Manager Graham Rix described him as the future of the club and dropped the veteran Dave Beasant to make way for his new signing.

But Rix was wrong. At 5 feet 10 inches, Kawaguchi was tall for a Japanese, but short for a goalkeeper in the English leagues. In fact, he was so concerned about his lack of height that he spiked his hair up to make himself look taller. It didn't work.

In 11 first-team starts, he picked the ball out of the net 21 times and kept only one clean sheet, which was against Stockport County.

After Portsmouth lost 4–1 to third division strugglers Leyton Orient at Fratton Park in the FA Cup, Kawaguchi was dropped. He would never start a game for Pompey again. In September 2003, Harry Redknapp, who had taken over as manager, allowed him to leave the club. It was 'sayonara' to a star of the east who failed to shine in the south.

SOUTHAMPTON

ALI DIA

Ali Dia will live long in the memory of Graeme Souness and all Southampton fans – even though his Saints career lasted all of 15 minutes in 1996.

Dia claimed to have been recommended by George Weah. He said they had been team-mates at Paris St Germain after Dia had moved from Bologna. He wasn't just a good club player though. He claimed that he had also played at international level with 13 caps for Senegal, and had scored twice in their most recent game. He talked himself up in the local press saying he had pace and could dribble well.

Duly impressed, Souness named him among his substitutes for their game against Leeds United at the Dell on November the 23rd. With things going poorly and Matthew Le Tissier injured, Souness gambled. He took off the Saints legend and replaced him with the triallist. Souness had reportedly never seen him play – and would never see him again.

A few poor early touches could be put down to nerves. But it quickly dawned on everyone that Dia was no international – just a world-class hoaxer. After 15 minutes, Dia missed an open goal and the manager had seen enough. The substitute was substituted. He was never seen at Southampton again. The truth was there was no recommendation from George Weah. No transfer from Bologna to PSG. His only competitive action had come at Croft Park where he made a single second half substitute appearance for Blyth Spartans.

His unforgettable cameo at the Dell wasn't the last English football saw of Ali Dia. A few days later he turned up at Gateshead. Three months later he was gone again, but in Southampton at least he will never be forgotten.

TOTTENHAM HOTSPUR

RAMON VEGA

Christian Gross famously brought a London underground ticket with him on his arrival at White Hart Lane. But contrary to popular perception, he didn't bring Ramon Vega with him.

The Swiss international defender was signed by Gerry Francis in 1997 from the Italian club Cagliari for £2.5 million. He would play more than 50 games for Spurs before he left for Celtic on a free. By that time he had firmly established himself as a player who was dangerous at both ends!

Vega became a figure of fun at White Hart Lane. Rival managers even ridiculed him. Before a Cup tie, Ron Noades, then Brentford chairman/manager said, 'You always know you have a chance when you see Ramon Vega run out.' Harsh words, especially as Brentford were struggling near the foot of the second division at the time.

Vega had a reputation for being one of the nicest guys in the game and clearly had Spurs' best interests at heart. But it wasn't enough to save him.

When he leapt high to concede a needless 12th-minute penalty at Stamford Bridge on the way to a crushing 3–0 defeat by Chelsea, it was effectively the end. By now Sol Campbell, Luke Young, Chris Perry and a youthful Ledley King were all ahead of him in the pecking order and George Graham, who had succeeded Gross, let him go.

Vega described his time at North London as depressing – but he had the last laugh. Vega went on to help Celtic complete the treble before moving on to first division strugglers Watford on a £25,000 a week contract.

While Christian Gross wasn't responsible for Vega, he did bring both Paulo Tremazzani and Nicola Berti to the Lane…

WEST BROMWICH ALBION

FRANZ CARR

Franz Carr was a footballing Concorde of the 80s and 90s – fast, but an expensive luxury.

He would fly past opposition defenders, but his fellow strikers would often be left frustrated as he would spray his crosses around like entries on a spot-the-ball coupon.

His most successful spell was early in his career at Nottingham Forest, but by the time he reached West Brom in 1998, after a brief unhappy spell in Italy with Reggiana, he was in the twilight of his career.

Carr started against Queens Park Rangers but was substituted during the match. He was on the bench on three other occasions but failed to get on the scoresheet. In fact Carr had never managed more than four goals in any of his 12 seasons in the English game.

West Brom were his last league club before he headed off to the United States to show opponents there a clean pair of heels while playing for the Pittsburgh Riverhounds.

THE CHAMPIONSHIP

The up-and-coming…

…and the been-and-gone

BRIGHTON & HOVE ALBION

GORDON SMITH

'And Smith must score…' is one of the most famous phrases in footballing history. Even though it was more than two decades ago, barely a day passes when the player involved isn't reminded of the moment when he failed to win the FA Cup for Brighton.

No one would suggest Gordon Smith is Brighton's worst player, but he was responsible for their worst moment.

Put clean through in the last minute of extra time in the 1983 final, he shot at goal…and hit Gary Bailey's legs. Manchester United held on for a replay which they duly won 4–0.

Brighton had never before and possibly will never in the future be as close to FA Cup glory.

Smith played in six FA Cup finals for Rangers and had actually scored Albion's first goal at Wembley, but it is his miss that has immortalised him.

Even Brighton's fanzine is still called 'And Smith Must Score…'

BURNLEY

BILLY O'ROURKE

Billy O'Rourke had waited patiently for his big chance. At Burnley in the late 1970s he was goalkeeping understudy to the ever-reliable, ever-present Alan Stevenson, who would eventually play 438 times for the club.

So when Stevenson was ruled out through injury for the first time in four seasons, O'Rourke knew he had to grab this rare opportunity with both hands. Sadly it slipped through his fingers.

His big day was at Loftus Road against Queens Park Rangers in 1979 – a game that was to be featured as the main match on BBC's *Match of the Day*.

After 90 minutes and seven goals past him, poor O'Rourke wept as he left the field. Even an over-generous 'Man of the Match' award from a local newspaper couldn't console him.

Stevenson was soon back and O'Rourke's chances were few and far between. He played another 13 times for Burnley before leaving in 1982.

That wasn't the end of his story though. Showing considerable character he put his debut horror story behind him and went on to build a career with both Blackpool and Tranmere Rovers.

Burnley's Billy O'Rourke can only watch the ball fly past him as he is caught off his line in an away game at Crystal Palace in 1983.

CARDIFF CITY

DAI THOMAS

A career that started so promisingly ended in disgrace for Cardiff striker Dai Thomas.

Graham Taylor had paid £100,000 to take the burly Welshman to Watford from Swansea, but it was a move that never worked out. A year and just three goals later he was packed off to Ninian Park in a half-price sale.

On the pitch, he struggled for goals and games. In the 1998–9 season he started 16 games for Cardiff, but was substituted in all but four. He also managed just four league goals. He started the first game of the 1999–2000 season, but was taken off at half-time and never re-established himself. The crowd who had once given him cult-hero status had turned against him as City plunged to relegation.

They would turn against him even more when a *Panorama* documentary alleged he was involved in riots in Brussels during Euro 2000.

Later he was jailed for 60 days after pleading guilty to threatening and violent behaviour after Cardiff's FA Cup win over Leeds United. His days as a professional footballer ended behind bars.

COVENTRY CITY

YSRAEL ZUNIGA

Like Paddington Bear, Ysrael Zuniga came from deepest Peru, wearing his warmest overcoat. The move from Lima to Leamington Spa was never likely to be easy.

With 32 goals in 26 games in his very first season at the top level in his native country, Ysrael had been South America's Golden Boot winner in 1999 when Gordon Strachan decided to take a chance on him at £800,000. He had only seen him on video and warned that he was one for the future, not the present.

The future at Coventry lasted three seasons which yielded just three goals. In that time City were relegated to the first division.

The inexperienced striker stood just 5 feet 8 inches tall and weighed a little over 11 stone. His nickname was 'The Little Hamster' – not likely to instil fear into the heart of most English defences.

Strachan described him as 'excellent inside the box, ordinary outside it'.

Sadly for him most Coventry fans felt he was just ordinary, and eventually he was allowed to return to Peru on a free transfer.

CREWE ALEXANDRA

DENNIS MURRAY

Crewe have long had a well-deserved reputation for producing high-quality players at Gresty Road – the likes of David Platt, Rob Jones, Danny Murphy, Seth Johnson and Robbie Savage are all relatively recent examples of those who have gone on to perform at the highest level.

Dennis Murray was not in that category… He made his debut as a teenager on September 29, 1951 – a date the young goalkeeper would never forget.

He conceded eleven goals as Crewe crashed 11–1 against Lincoln City in the Third Division North, which is still the club's record league defeat. In an act of amazing faith, Murray kept his place in the side and responded by playing his part in a 2–1 win over Chesterfield.

Despite this result Dennis Murray never played league football again. No photographs of Murray in action are in existence, so the keeper he was never good enough to replace, Peter Ellson, is pictured here instead.

DERBY COUNTY

ESTEBAN FUERTES

Derby County have had some unpopular overseas strikers in their time – Mikkel Beck and Fabrizio Ravanelli to name just two.

Esteban Fuertes barely had time to become unpopular. In one of the strangest episodes in Derby's history, the Argentinian striker finally signed from Colon De Santa Fe for more than £2 million after four months of wrangling over red tape. He scored on his home debut, but in his eight Premiership starts that was the only goal he mustered. He often looked distracted and off the pace, which wasn't really surprising as he was in England on a forged passport.

Fuertes had claimed he had Italian grandparents. But when he tried to get back into England after a club trip to Portugal, he was refused entry by immigration officials at Heathrow. He never played for Derby again. His stay had yielded eight starts, one goal and one red card… or two if you count the one given by the immigration department.

GILLINGHAM

DAVID QUIRKE

Scoring that first league goal is a sweet never-to-be forgotten moment. But for some players it never arrives, try as they may. David Quirke tried for more than six years at Gillingham between 1967 and 1973. The big Irishman was a reliable and regular member of the defence, but, however hard he tried, he couldn't get on the scoresheet. Not with his feet or head, not with knee or his chest, not even off his backside. By the time he left the club he'd gone a Lundekvamesque 230 games without managing a single league goal. He never played league football again so he never enjoyed that euphoric moment.

Perhaps it's something in the Gillingham air because full-back Paul Haylock suffered a similar fate. He had scored for his previous club, Norwich. He scored for his next club, Maidstone United…and his next, Shrewsbury Town. But in 152 games for the Priestfield side he didn't get one goal.

IPSWICH TOWN

FINIDI GEORGE

Finidi George kissed the girls at Portman Road, but made them – and all Ipswich Town fans – cry after a spell in East Anglia that promised so much, but delivered precious little.

The flying Nigerian, who could run 100 metres in under 11 seconds, was almost as quick off the mark when he joined the club from Real Mallorca, scoring in the first quarter of an hour in his debut against Derby County. He would later score a second goal and memorably kiss an exultant female fan in the crowd. It makes a change from kissing the badge!

The £3 million George Burley had spent and the reported £20,000 a week wages looked well spent. But within months Finidi lost his form and broke his jaw; Ipswich were relegated; Burley was sacked and the £20,000 a week didn't look so well spent after all.

New manager Joe Royle didn't rate the Nigerian, but Ipswich – by now in dire financial straits – couldn't get rid of him.

In the end Ipswich paid him to go, possibly as much as £1 million, after just seven league goals in two seasons.

A super-eagle who turned out to be anything but super.

LEEDS UNITED

TOMAS BROLIN

Tomas Brolin is rated as Sweden's finest-ever footballer...and Leeds United's worst.

In 1994 he was ranked in the top three footballers in Europe and had been nicknamed 'The Swedish Maradona'. He was graceful, skilful and captivating at his peak, and football fans in this country still remember the fine goal he scored for Sweden against England in Euro 92.

George Graham gave Elland Road fans the chance to see Brolin at first hand by signing him from Parma for £4.5 million. In fact they couldn't miss him – there was a lot of him. The *Observer* described him as looking like Keith Chegwin's tubby twin, and opposition fans enjoyed taunting him with 'Who Ate All the Pies?'.

Out of shape and out of form, the Swede would make just 19 appearances in two seasons for Leeds. He complained that the manager had said only two words to him in that time – though he's not revealing which two they were. Eventually he was loaned to the Swiss club FC Zurich but refused to return to Yorkshire when the loan spell ended, despite threats of legal action against him.

Leeds eventually paid him off, though he would return to England for an equally unsuccessful spell with Crystal Palace.

Eight years after scoring against England, Brolin was selling vacuum cleaners in his native Sweden and later opened a nightclub in Stockholm.

There has been stern competition for the tag of Leeds' worst-ever player in recent times. Brazilian World Cup winner Jose Vitor Roque Junior arrived in September 2003. In his first five games in defence, Leeds conceded 20 goals and manager Peter Reid lost his job.

But no one can quite match their heavyweight midfield Tomas Brolin.

LEICESTER CITY

FRANK SINCLAIR

More and more footballers these days have letters after their name – CBEs, MBEs and OBEs have all been awarded for services to football.

Frank Sinclair also often has letters after his name – OG.

It may seem harsh to include Sinclair in this list. After all, he played more than 200 games for Chelsea and nearly as many for City. He was also once voted Leicester's 'Player of the Season'. Many instead would nominate Ade Akinbiyi, who after a rare Foxes goal against Sunderland ripped off his shirt to reveal a male model body. City fans believed he had missed his true vocation. Or Trevor Benjamin who managed just 10 goals in his 81 league games for City after his £1.5 million move from Cambridge. But for being in the wrong place at the wrong time, on and off the pitch, Sinclair takes some beating.

Frank announced his arrival at City from Chelsea with two goals in three games at the start of the 1999–2000 season. Unfortunately they were both against his own side. At Highbury on the opening day of the season, City were seconds away from a point against Arsenal when Sinclair swung his foot at the ball in a goalmouth scramble, sending it flying past the startled Tim Flowers. And it was again in the last minute that he put through his own goal against Chelsea – when Leicester were leading 2–1.

His most spectacular strike came in 2002 against Middlesbrough when he curled a 40 yarder beyond Ian Walker after just three minutes. In his time with the club he managed three at the right end and three at the wrong end.

It has not just been on the field that Sinclair has had his problems. Martin O'Neill sent him home 24 hours before the 1999 Worthington Cup final for a breach of club discipline. At the time O'Neill said, 'everyone deserves five, six or seven chances but after 77 you blot your copybook'.

There was also an inevitability in the final game of the 2003–4 season, with City doing their level best to stop Arsenal going through the season unbeaten, it would be Sinclair who would upend Thierry Henry for the decisive penalty. It was his last act as a City player. Sinclair was released at the end of the season.

MILLWALL

SERGEI YURAN

No one liked him. And he didn't care. Sergei Yuran arrived at Millwall from Spartak Moscow in 1996 along with his fellow countryman Vassili Kulkov.

By the time they left the manager Mick McCarthy had gone and the club had been relegated and was on the verge of financial ruin.

The pair, both considered heroes in Russia, had been paid £150,000 each to sign for the club and £5,000 a week to transform the struggling south-east London club. But of the 13 games that Yuran started, Millwall won just three. And he managed just one goal in that time.

Kulkov made a paltry six appearances. The pair were seen more often in the pubs of the Old Kent Road than at the Den – Yuran even managed to pick up a drink driving conviction during his brief stay in England.

McCarthy's successor Jimmy Nicholl showed them the door. Yuran he said was 'an embarrassment to himself and the club. He contributed the worst level of commitment I have even seen.' So much for Millwall's Russian revolution.

NOTTINGHAM FOREST

JASON LEE

Curly perms, blond rinses, shaven scalps, mohicans – the game has seen every possible hairstyle over the years. But it has never seen anything quite like Jason Lee.

Lee's goalscoring record at Nottingham Forest was such that he might have been advised to keep a low profile. Instead he sported a pineapple-style creation, which got him both noticed and ridiculed.

Crowds loved chanting the highly original 'He's got a pineapple on his head' to the tune of 'He's got the whole world in his hands'.

It did nothing for Jason's fragile confidence in front of goal. In his four seasons at the City ground, he scored two, five, eight and one goal respectively, before eventually moving on to Watford for £200,000.

The pineapple-cut may be long gone, but the player isn't. He was still playing in the 2003–4 season for Falkirk in the Scottish first division. With almost 400 league appearances to his credit in England and Scotland, perhaps Jason Lee has had the last laugh.

PLYMOUTH ARGYLE

PAUL BOARDMAN

Peter Shilton's judgement when he was a goalkeeper was never questioned. But as a manager, it was a different matter!

Among his first signings as manager of Plymouth Argyle was a young 6 foot striker from non-league Knowsley United called Paul Boardman, son of the scouse comedian, Stan.

Boardman had a dream debut three months after signing when he got the first goal in a 2–1 win over Bournemouth at Home Park.

Despite that he didn't play again until April in a 3–0 defeat by local rivals Exeter City.

Paul was on the bench at Blackpool at the start of the following season, but injuries wrecked his career. He decided to follow in his father's footsteps instead, and for eight years was a stand-up comedian. No doubt, this entry will severely test his sense of humour.

Now, instead of playing football, he talks about it as a presenter on Sky Sports.

TONY LORMOR

PRESTON NORTH END

TONY LORMOR

Preston North End fans loved David Reeves – and that was a problem for Tony Lormor.

Lormor was a journeyman pro, doing well at virtually every club he played for. But when he moved to Deepdale as part of a deal that took the popular Reeves to Chesterfield, it was soon obvious his face didn't fit.

Lormor himself would admit that he wasn't the quickest on the pitch, and to this day Preston fans claim he is the only striker who lost height when he jumped! It's probably a good job home supporters didn't dish out the same type of abuse to a young David Beckham when he was briefly there on loan from Manchester United – otherwise English footballing history could be very different.

Lormor scored on his debut for his new club, but despite that was given only three months before he was shipped out on loan to Notts County. He didn't play for Preston again, but was sold first to Mansfield and then to Hartlepool.

QUEENS PARK RANGERS

NED ZELIC

There have been many Australian success stories in English football, but Ned Zelic was not one of them. Queens Park Rangers' fans still wince at the mention of the giant defender's name.

Zelic arrived at Loftus Road in 1995 as the club invested some of the £6 million they had received for Les Ferdinand from Newcastle United.

In theory Zelic was a ball-playing libero, but supporters never really got the chance to see if he could put this theory into practice.

Within weeks of his arrival in West London, he was in hospital with knee trouble. When he recovered, he played three times in the Premiership, none of which ended in a win. He was promptly loaned to Eintracht Frankfurt who were relegated that season – just like Rangers.

Zelic never played in English football again, but went on to prove his value with 1860 Munich and was still playing in Japan, injury free, in the 2003–4 season.

At Rangers though, he's still regarded as a 'Shepherd's bushwacker'!

READING

BORIS MIKHAILOV

Perhaps it was the constant media attention given to his wig that unsettled goalkeeper Borislav 'Bobby' Mikhailov during his time at Reading. After all the Bulgarian had been one of the outstanding performers in the 1994 World Cup in the United States – the first time he appeared with a full head of hair after being totally bald.

Perhaps it was a communication problem. Bobby spoke no English, his defenders no Bulgarian.

Mikhailov managed 16 appearances in his first season, alternating with Simon Sheppard. But his second season would be his nadir.

In the second game of the season, he was red-carded at Ipswich with the sides level at 1–1. Reading went on to lose 5–2.

After his suspension, he returned in September to play in a 6–1 home defeat by Crystal Palace! That was the last Reading fans saw of him until January when he was dropped again after letting in four goals at Birmingham. He would play just once more for the club – an injury sustained against Bolton ended his back-breaking spell in English football.

ROTHERHAM UNITED

GIJSBERT BOS

Holland has produced some marvellous footballers over the years and many – Arnold Muhren, Franz Thijssen, Johnny Metgod, Denis Bergkamp, Ruud van Nistelrooy and a host of others – have graced the English leagues.

In the view of Rotherham United fans Gijsbert Bos did not grace the English leagues, not even the third division which is where they were when the giant Dutchman played for them. The Millmoor faithful still regularly vote for him as their worst-ever player.

It had all started so promisingly for the 6 feet 4 inches tall striker after his move from Lincoln City. He scored four goals in the first two months of the season – admittedly all of them from close range.

But after September he barely played and never scored again.

Bos was loaned to Walsall where he was known as 'The Lost Man'. He never played and soon after disappeared without trace from the English game.

Gijsbert Bos

SHEFFIELD UNITED

BILLY WHITEHURST

Billy Whitehurst was what was euphemistically known as 'an old-fashioned centre forward'. He terrorised defences, but not with his goals or ability. His first touch was usually with his elbow or knee! As the former Scottish international defender Colin Calderwood admitted, he would have preferred playing against Ronaldo than Whitehurst, who had treated him like 'a rag-doll'.

Whitehurst was the hardest man in the game in the late 1980s. His colourful career was taken to the top level at Newcastle United where his attempts to follow in the footsteps of Jackie Milburn, Wyn Davies and Malcolm McDonald made him unpopular with the St James' Park crowd.

He was signed by Sheffield United in 1990 – even though he had once hung club director Dave Capper on an office door – as cover for Brian Deane and Tony Agana. He only scored twice in a year with the club, and put the opposing keeper in the back of the net as often as the ball.

Whitehurst only managed one more career goal after leaving Sheffield United, before taking over the running of a pub. Aptly perhaps, it was called the Butcher's Arms.

STOKE CITY

KYLE LIGHTBOURNE

Sometimes a nickname tells the whole story. Bermudan international striker Kyle Lightbourne had been a big favourite at Walsall, with his goals earning him a £500,000 move to Coventry, swiftly followed by a transfer to Stoke City for the same fee.

After four seasons in which the 6 feet 2 inches tall striker failed to reach double figures, City fans would for ever remember him, cruelly, as Kyle Lightweight. It didn't help that he had done so well for local rivals Walsall, or that Stoke were relegated to the second division during his spell there.

Loan spells at Swindon and Cardiff failed to help him find his goalscoring touch, so he dropped to the third division with Macclesfield. He managed just four goals for his new club – a poor return from their highest-ever paid player. Despite that one supporter's website lists him in the Silkmen's greatest ever side – or on the bench to be precise!

SUNDERLAND

MILTON NUNEZ

It takes something special to oust Lillian Laslandes as Sunderland's worst-ever player. They spent £3.6 million on the French international, who managed just a dozen goalless appearances before the Wearsiders finally managed to unload him.

But Milton Nunez was special. The Honduran international was intended to provide competition for strikers Niall Quinn and Kevin Phillips. The club paid £1.6 million for him, rising to £2.6 million depending on appearances.

Yet when Peter Reid's new man was unveiled to the crowd, the fans were unsure whether to laugh or cry.

Nunez stood just 5 feet 5 inches tall. He could not even reach the top shelf in north-east supermarkets to do his shopping. There was speculation that the club had bought the 'wrong' Milton Nunez.

The Nunez they had got managed just one appearance as a substitute before returning to South America. The only consolation was that Sunderland would never have to pay the extra million...

WATFORD

PIERRE ISSA

Famously and foolishly in June 2001, Gianluca Vialli promised to make Watford 'The Manchester United of Division One'. He paid big money to bring in a host of big names, including former AC Milan defender Filippo Galli, Ramon Vega from Celtic, and from Marseille Patrick Blondeau and experienced South African international defender Pierre Issa.

By June 2002, Vialli and his assistant Ray Wilkins had been sacked and players were being asked to take wage deferrals to help the club out of its financial mess.

Fans had no doubt where the blame lay. They voted Issa captain of a worst-ever Watford XI.

In Issa's second match, Norwich City's Iwan Roberts terrorised him – and he never seemed to regain his confidence. In his first five games, often, frighteningly, paired with Vega in the heart of the defence, Watford conceded 13 goals.

Issa was dropped – twice. Firstly by stretcher bearers as they carried him off after he had dislocated his shoulder against Birmingham City, and then by Vialli. His stay in England was short and painful for all concerned.

WEST HAM UNITED

MARCO BOOGERS

Harry Redknapp openly admits he had never seen Marco Boogers play when he agreed to pay £1 million to Sparta Rotterdam in July 1995. When the Dutch striker left West Ham three years later, he still hadn't seen him play – well, barely.

Boogers was reckoned to be the third best player in Holland and Redknapp thought he had discovered a world-beater.

It turned out he had signed the Hammers' worst-ever player. Boogers reportedly didn't speak a word of English – though in training he understood enough to demand the ball at his feet. Running was certainly not in his vocabulary.

He failed to make a single start, though he did make his mark on Gary Neville when he was red carded for an horrendous foul on the player during a brief substitute appearance against Manchester United.

Boogers famously disappeared, only to emerge weeks later, living in a caravan park in Holland and claiming 'I am not mental'. West Ham fans disagreed dubbing him 'Mad' Marco before he was packed off on a free transfer to Groningen.

Redknapp vowed never to buy again after this particular video nasty unless he had seen the footballer play live.

WIGAN ATHLETIC

JORG SMEETS

Good things come in small packages – sometimes. Jorg Smeets is the shortest player ever to play for Wigan Athletic. No one is quite sure how short as he never revealed his actual height. The best guess was between 5 feet 4 inches and 5 feet 5 inches, but Smeets was so tiny he had to have his boots specially made.

You may think the English second division would not be the best place for a diddy Dutchman, and you would be right. Despite that Wigan paid £100,000 to Dutch club Heracles in October 1997.

Three days later he made his debut at Grimsby's Blundell Park where he discovered the meaning of 'clogging' in English!

The majority of his year-and-a-half stay was spent on the bench, though he did manage three goals for the club, none of them headers!

Of course size doesn't always matter. Middlesbrough's wonderful Brazilian Juninho is just 5 feet 5 inches tall!

WOLVERHAMPTON WANDERERS

ISAAC OKORONKWO

Defender Isaac Okoronkwo arrived in England by the most unorthodox route imaginable.

The Nigerian international, who reputedly modelled his game on the great Italian Franco Baresi, had played his football in Qatar, Lebanon, Moldova and Ukraine. So Wolves manager Dave Jones was quietly confident about him when he signed Okoronkwo from Shaktar Donetsk before the start of the 2003–4 season. 'If he can settle in the Ukraine, he should settle here' said Jones. He was wrong.

The man brought in to bolster the Midlander's first season at the top level for 20 years didn't play at all in the Premiership until the middle of April.

His problems began even before a ball was kicked. Due to difficulties with his international clearance he didn't play in the pre-season games. Then he picked up a hamstring injury which kept him out of the reckoning for the next two months.

When the Molineux management team did get a first-hand look at what they had, they were not overly impressed.

'I am fast when I do not have the ball,' said Isaac. The problem was when he did have the ball. Then he was ponderous and uncertain – not much of the Baresi about him.

It probably didn't impress the coaching team either when he admitted that when he wasn't playing he enjoyed snooker, video games and 'a little booze'. Wolves were certainly punch-drunk by the time Okoronkwo got his first-team chance in a 3–3 draw against Manchester City.

In fact, he played in the last seven games of the season – but the damage was done. Wolves were relegated back to the first division and Okoronkwo was sent packing, doubtless to another far-flung footballing frontier.

LEAGUE ONE
& LEAGUE TWO

The wannabees, the never-will-bees…

…and the just couldn't-be-bothered-to-bees.

BARNSLEY

GEORGI HRISTOV

Any un-popularity contest in Barnsley would have only one winner. Every woman in the town would vote for Macedonian international Georgi Hristov. Quite a few of the men would too.

In two years the club's record signing was on the scoresheet just eight times – but also managed one massive own goal.

Hristov, who cost £1.5 million from Partizan Belgrade, said publicly that Barnsley girls were 'ugly' and drank 'too much beer'. From that moment, he could have scored 30 goals a season. It still wouldn't have made him popular.

The club said that the comments had been exaggerated. Presumably he had meant 'quite ugly'.

Hristov was perceived as being lazy and sullen by the club's fans. Barnsley were relegated from the Premiership and after two seasons Hristov was given a free transfer.

Ironically he scored seven times in his first three games for his new club NEC Nijmegen.

BLACKPOOL

TONY DIAMOND

Ted McDougall scored goals for every club he played for – except Blackpool! At Bournemouth, York, Norwich, West Ham, Southampton and even Manchester United he got on the scoresheet. Blackpool was his last club – thirteen goalless games doubtless encouraging him to hang up his boots.

Tony Diamond did score in one of the handful of games he played for the club in 1989 – and yet gets the Blackpool vote by a hair's breadth.

Many of the Bloomfield Road faithful felt that the ex-Blackburn man was reluctant to head the ball due to his carefully coiffured hair. Some fans claim that despite their increasingly vocal encouragement during his stay at the club he failed to head the ball even once.

BOSTON UNITED

STEVE BURTON

When Boston United wanted a bright, young, energetic striker for their first season as a Football League club, they decided to sign Steve Burton on loan from Ipswich Town.

He started their away game at Wrexham in August 2002, but was substituted. He started the next game at home to Lincoln, but again was taken off. It was a pattern that became monotonously repetitious for Burton. He started six league games for United – but didn't complete any of them before his loan spell was cut short.

He then moved to his home-town club, Doncaster Rovers, in April 2003 and scored a goal for them in the Conference. But he started only one third division game. And, you're right, he was substituted in it.

Burton was given a free transfer at the end of the 2003–4 season having still never completed the full 90 minutes in the Football League.

GEORGE LAWRENCE

BOURNEMOUTH

GEORGE LAWRENCE

It was Danny Wallace at Southampton who penned the nickname Chicken George for one of his team-mates – and it stuck.

Years after it was first used, Bournemouth fans would still call flying right winger George Lawrence by his foul nickname.

Manager Harry Redknapp took Lawrence to Dean Court for £100,000 in 1989 – a hefty amount for the club both then and now. But his electrifying pace rarely produced electrifying goals – he scored just five in 75 appearances. Fans remember him often racing past opposition full-backs only to put his crosses over the bar or over his team-mates.

When his days on the south coast ended, he played in Finland and Malta, presumably in the hope of getting rid of that nickname. Nowadays Lawrence is a qualified sports therapist and FIFA agent.

BRADFORD CITY

JUANJO

Benito Carbone and Stan Collymore cost Bradford City dearly as the club tried unsuccessfully to buy its way to Premiership safety in 2001.

But for sheer underachievement Juanjo's spell at Valley Parade takes some beating.

His timing was certainly bad – the club was on the brink of administration and manager Jim Jeffries was about to get the sack. Teaming up again with his former Heart's boss had been the main reason for the Spaniard's move.

Still, he scored on his debut against Walsall – his first and his last goal for the club.

With Nicky Law in charge, Juanjo's opportunites would be few and far between. In his second season he had to wait until November for a start. City lost 3–0 to Nottingham Forest. He kept his place for the next game. City lost 5–0 to Sheffield United.

Juanjo never played for City again, and was freed when his contract ran out.

BRENTFORD

GUS HURDLE

It was anything but fantasy football for Brentford defender Gus Hurdle when he appeared alongside comedians Frank Skinner and David Baddiel to demonstrate his ball-juggling skills. He managed just two keepy-uppies – less than Danny Baker – and fans never let him forget it.

Hurdle, who joined the club from Dorchester Town, was regarded as 'too nice' by many Brentford supporters during his 90-game goalless career, which was spread over five seasons.

Eventually he was released by new manager Micky Adams and settled for a combination of non-league and World Cup football! Hurdle played for Egham, Dulwich, Crawley, Molesey and Barbados. However, his international career ended when he was sent off after 38 minutes during a 7–0 defeat in a World Cup qualifier against the United States.

Gus wasn't put off television by his earlier embarrassment – far from it. He went on to work as a production assistant on BBC2's *Food and Drink*.

STEVE JONES

BRISTOL CITY

STEVE JONES

When he joined Bristol City in September 1999, Steve Jones knew he was a stone-and-a-half overweight. What he didn't know was that, while he could lose the weight, he couldn't lose the stigma of being signed by Tony Pulis.

Pulis, who had paid £425,000 for the former Bournemouth, West Ham and Charlton striker, was reviled by many City fans and would soon leave the club. During his debut against Millwall, Jones was shocked by the abuse hurled at the manager and began to realise the fans could easily make life difficult for him too. Short of fitness and form, he managed just two goals in 14 games and within four months of joining was loaned out to Brentford and then Southend.

Worse was to follow. He broke his foot in September 2000 and failed to make a single first-team appearance for City that season. Jones would score a handful of goals for City – then under Danny Wilson – in the 2001–2 season. But City fans had made up their minds. In a poll, 41 per cent voted him their worst-ever player.

231

ROBBIE TURNER

BRISTOL ROVERS

ROBBIE TURNER

Bristol Rovers have had some terrific strikers. Nathan Ellington, Jason Roberts, Marcus Stewart and Jamie Cureton all had spells at the club before going on to score at a higher level.

Robbie Turner never quite came into that category. Rovers were one of a dozen clubs he played for in a career that took him the length and breadth of the country – but only once did he reach double figures for a season during the halcyon days of his career at Plymouth.

His time at Twerton Park was spread over two seasons during 1987. He scored once in his first season. And once in his second.

Turner spent the next year at Wimbledon, where he failed to score at all.

Despite that he was still earning a crust from the game until he joined Hull City on loan in 1996. He scored twice with headers on his debut before being ruled out by an injury sustained while sneezing in bed!

BURY

MARK 'CARLO' SERTORI

Mark 'Carlo' Sertori is remembered by Bury fans as a ten-minute hero.

He had already had spells at Stockport, Lincoln and Wrexham before arriving at Gigg Lane in July 1994. Sertori was a man mountain, 6 feet 2 inches tall and weighing in at more than 14 stone.

Bizarrely he was rumoured to own an ice-cream van to supplement his income between matches. He had plenty of time to do just that. In his first season he made only two substitute appearances.

Sertori finally got his first start in September 1995, shoring up the Bury defence in a 2–2 draw with Lincoln. But a home defeat by Cambridge in the next game saw him dropped.

When he re-emerged in April it was in the unlikely role as striker! Just 10 minutes had gone when Sertori scored his first – and last – Bury goal as they defeated Fulham.

When Sertori was released at the end of his second season he had started just four league matches.

CAMBRIDGE UNITED

DEVON WHITE

It was always going to be difficult following in the size nine footsteps of Dion Dublin at Cambridge United, who had been sold for £1 million to Manchester United before the start of the 1992–3 season.

The task fell to the willing Devon White. Like Dublin he stood well over 6 feet tall. And while Dublin had been scoring for Cambridge, White had been prolific at Bristol Rovers. But as far as the Abbey Stadium faithful were concerned there was no comparison.

It wasn't just the new man who was failing to hit the target – it was the whole team. They lost their first three games without scoring and White was dropped.

He did finally get off the mark in October during a defeat by Derby County, but the club's patience was running out.

When they paid a club record fee to re-sign Steve Claridge from Luton in November, the writing was on the wall. White was sold to Queens Park Rangers and went on to play for Notts County, Watford and Shrewsbury. He scored goals for them all – but at Cambridge United, Devon was far from glorious.

CHELTENHAM TOWN

JASON WHITE

Jason White scored goals while at Scunthorpe. He scored goals at Scarborough, Northampton and Rotherham too.

But hard as he tried, he could not score for Cheltenham Town.

Legend has it that dogs in the animal shelter next to Whaddon Road ran for cover when Jason took aim.

In 27 games for Cheltenham in the 2000–2001 season, his first at the club, the man who had hit the target wherever he had been, failed to score at all. He went on loan to Mansfield where, in seven games, he also failed to score.

At the end of the season he was transfer listed by manager Steve Cotterill, but there were no takers and he started the following season on the bench for the home game against Leyton Orient.

In the 64th minute it happened – White came off the bench and scored the equaliser. Home fans cheered disbelievingly, while the canine neighbours breathed sighs of relief. It turned out to be his only goal for Cheltenham. He was freed at the end of the season and headed for a new life in Singapore.

CHESTER CITY

WALE KWIK-AJET

Never has a fleet-footed forward been better named than Wale Kwik-Ajet. Unfortunately for him, he was never given the chance to show his paces in Chester City's first team.

Kwik-Ajet was the first signing of chairman-turned-coach Terry Smith, who believed training techniques could be transferred from American gridiron to soccer. They couldn't. Chester fans hated Smith, and his buys were tainted by association.

Kwik-Ajet was No. 27 in a first-team squad sponsored by Kwik Save (honestly) but was never good enough to make the first team, even in a side that was nosediving into the Conference.

Instead he played in a handful of reserve games in 2000 – a goal in a 3–2 win over Rochdale reserves in the Pontins League Division Two, turned out to be the highlight of his time at the Deva.

He headed to Scotland where he combined brief spells with Queen's Park, Hamilton and Cowdenbeath with his job selling Sky TV dishes, before returning to England to play for Hednesford Town.

He may never have been great, but he was Kwik!

CHESTERFIELD

MIKE ASTBURY

Chesterfield have long had a reputation for fine goalkeepers. It was where the great Gordon Banks played his first league football.

But in the 1988–9 season they were struggling to replace long-serving, reliable Jim Brown who had played more than 180 times for the club.

In the end they plumped for Mike Astbury from Chester City. He played only a handful of games for Chesterfield – but has the worst record of goals conceded per game of any of the club's post-war keepers, letting in 20 goals in eight starts.

Astbury started well enough in a victory over Aldershot, but 3–0 defeats by Wolves and Northampton followed, and after a 5–0 defeat by Port Vale he was dropped.

The beleaguered keeper was eventually recalled, only to concede six goals at Preston.

Chesterfield were relegated to the fourth division and Astbury was released. He would never play league football again.

COLCHESTER UNITED

ROY McDONOUGH

The red mist occasionally descends on some players, and Roy McDonough spent his whole career in a disciplinary pea-souper! The striker was sent off 21 times – a record in England. Several of those dismissals were during his two spells at Colchester United.

His first red card for them came aptly on Boxing Day in 1982 in a flare-up with Peterborough's Neil Firm, who took his revenge by scoring the winner.

After spells with Southend, Exeter and Cambridge United, he marked his return to Layer Road by being sent off in his first match back.

As player-manager, he steered Colchester back into the Football League – and celebrated by being red carded in their fourth game back (against Shrewsbury) and later in the season (against Rochdale). By now his style was being adopted by his team-mates with the club fined £7,500 after picking up 68 bookings in their first 29 games.

Despite it all McDonough made 500 league appearances – how many more might it have been?

DARLINGTON

JOHN WILLIAMS

The Flying Postman was unquestionably fast, but he didn't always deliver goals.

John Williams sprang to prominence in a *Saint & Greavsie* competition to find the quickest player in the league. Williams was at Coventry at the time – the highpoint of his career. But even there you could list his goals on the back of a stamp – just 11 in three years.

Despite that he was unquestionably popular at most of his many clubs – he went to Wycombe, Hereford, Walsall, Exeter, Cardiff and York before arriving at Darlington just before Christmas 2000.

Williams scored just once in his first 13 games and finished with five for the season as the Quakers slumped to 20th in the third division. At the end of the season, he was on the move again to Swansea and then Kidderminster Harriers.

Ironically he returned to Darlington to help spoil the party when they opened their new ground, the Reynolds Arena, playing for Harriers in their 2–0 win.

JOHN RYAN

DONCASTER ROVERS

JOHN RYAN

The man who is beyond question Doncaster Rovers' worst-ever player never actually kicked a ball for them.

John Ryan made one substitute appearance for the Yorkshire side in stoppage time in their Conference game against Hereford United. Manager Dave Penney introduced the newcomer three minutes from time at Edgar Street, and even though he failed to get a single touch, Ryan said he was 'over the moon' with his performance.

No one would have argued if he had got the Man of the Match award, because the unlikely debutant was also Rovers' owner and chairman.

At just a month short of his 53rd birthday Ryan also went into the record books as the oldest player to turn out for a professional club, beating the record set by Neil McBain of New Brighton in 1947.

The reaction of Richard O'Kelly, the player who was dropped from the bench to make way for Ryan, is not on record!

GRIMSBY TOWN

ASHLEY FICKLING

Grimsby is famous for fish and chicken. Fish because it's still a working port, while Ivano Bonetti will for ever be remembered as the player whose jaw was broken by flying chicken (or at least by the plate carrying the chicken and allegedly thrown by his frustrated manager).

Bonetti was one of a handful of glamorous-sounding imports to play for the club, as were Enzo Gambaro and Knut Anders Fostervold.

Ashley Fickling didn't sound glamorous and he wasn't. He was a Sheffield born and bred defender and had been on the books at Bramall Lane. So he will have shared Grimsby fans' horror as he dived to head a never-to-be-forgotten full-length own goal against Sheffield Wednesday in the 1996–7 season. Almost as bad, the Mariners lost the game 7–1.

In his 39 Grimsby games Fickling managed just two at the right end.

Things got no more glamorous for Fickling... he was transferred to Scunthorpe United.

HARTLEPOOL UNITED

CLIFF WRIGHT

There have of course been no poor players at Hartlepool. As a supporter of 40 years' standing, I write from a position of authority.

Few players in my lifetime though were given more unmerciful criticism from the Victoria Park terraces than Cliff Wright.

Wright was an inside forward in the days when there were inside forwards. He played more than 180 games for the club, many of them under Brian Clough, and scored 31 league goals.

Yet from almost his first game to his last he was known by the fans as 'Mary', and they would demand to know why he had forgotten his handbag. As the crowd was within touching distance of the players, there can be no question that he knew of his nickname. It was hardly designed to help his confidence or performances. I never understood why he became 'Mary' and I still don't. He wasn't a bad player, because as I've explained, there have been no bad players at Hartlepool!

CLIFF
WRIGHT

HUDDERSFIELD TOWN

GEORGE DONIS

Steve Bruce has a fantastic record in the transfer market, but he may not remember his first signing as Huddersfield boss with much affection.

On the face of it taking George Donis to the McAlpine Stadium was a bit of a coup. He had played at the very highest level in Greece, numbering nearly 150 games for Panathinaikos and AEK Athens.

In theory he cost Huddersfield nothing as he arrived on a Bosman. In practice it is estimated the club paid out a million pounds in various fees, not to mention wages. What's a Greek urn? A great deal, in this case! Donis would never repay his manager's faith.

Loss of form combined with injuries meant Donis made just 10 starts for Huddersfield and completed the 90 minutes only four times – hardly enough time for the fans to nickname him 'Donkey'. As Huddersfield Town slipped out of the promotion race, so Donis slipped out of the league. His last appearance was in a goalless draw against Grimsby. He was subbed after just 54 minutes and not seen in blue-and-white stripes again.

HULL CITY

MARK HATELEY

Football is a funny game! A player who graced some of Europe's finest clubs was once named Hull City's worst-ever player with 28 per cent of the votes cast.

Mark Hateley had a glittering career with Rangers, AC Milan and Monaco. He even won 32 caps for England. But by the time he was appointed player-manager at Boothferry Park, 'Attila' wasn't quite as rampant as he had been in his younger days.

As well as scoring goals, he also had the problem of producing a winning team. Now 35, Hateley didn't manage either.

He played just a handful of games in his first season, even though the team struggled desperately, finishing 22nd in division three.

He finally scored his first goal for Hull more than a year after his debut – from the penalty spot against Chester. His only goal from open play came two months later, shortly before he was sacked, with Hull in 92nd position in the Football League.

Hateley decided that he had had enough and quit the game to work in the media in Scotland.

KIDDERMINSTER HARRIERS

DYLAN KERR

Dylan Kerr's Kidderminster Harriers' career was all washed up after just three minutes.

He joined the club in September 2000 after successful spells at Reading and Kilmarnock and made the briefest of debuts as a late substitute in the third division game against Leyton Orient. After the match the streaked-haired defender headed back to Scotland ostensibly to wash his clothes. When he rang to ask manager Jan Molby if he could miss training and take an extra day's break, he was sacked. 'We are a friendly club, but not a holiday camp', said the great Dane.

In some respects it was typical of Maltese-born Kerr who Kilmarnock fans described as 'mad but loveable'.

After Aggborough, he had spells at Clydebank, Morton, Hamilton and East Stirling. More recently he has been coaching youngsters in Phoenix, Arizona. He no longer goes home to do his washing!

LEYTON ORIENT

GARY FLETCHER

It was what Rodney Marsh would describe as a knee-jerk reaction. Manager Tommy Taylor was impressed when Northwich Victoria striker Gary Fletcher scored twice against his Leyton Orient side. So impressed, he agreed to pay around £75,000 for the player in the summer of 2001.

Unfortunately, while Fletcher had no problem scoring against Orient, he couldn't score for them.

It was almost two years later when he finally managed to break his duck in the league, scoring a late equaliser at Torquay.

He joined Lincoln City on a free in the summer of 2003, teaming up again with his old boss at Northwich, Keith Alexander. The goals that had dried up so dramatically soon began to flow. He finished the season as top scorer with 19 goals.

And Orient fans who never saw him score a league goal at Brisbane Road, finally did. He got both goals as Lincoln won there 2-0 in March.

ADAM BUCKLEY

LINCOLN CITY

ADAM BUCKLEY

It is never easy following in a famous father's footsteps – just ask Calum Best, whose dad wasn't too shabby!

It's proved far from easy for Adam Buckley, whose three clubs – West Bromwich Albion, Grimsby Town and Lincoln City – have all been managed by his dad, Alan. In truth Adam had only been a schoolboy at the Hawthorns and his dad could hardly be accused of nepotism at Grimsby where he gave his son only a handful of starts.

It wasn't easy for Adam though as the crowd would chant, 'What do we do with the other Buckley?' to the tune of 'What do we do with a drunken sailor?'.

When Alan moved to Lincoln City in 2001, Adam soon followed. The combination fared no better. Adam started 19 games from midfield that season, but City won just one of them and finished 22nd in division three.

Buckley senior left at the end of that season. Though Adam stayed, he never started another league game for the club. In 49 career league appearances he had never scored a goal.

HERVE BACQUE

LUTON TOWN

HERVE BACQUE

It all ended in tears at Luton for French striker Herve Bacque.

Given the chance to score his first goal in English football against Walsall in the Auto Windscreen Shield, he produced what fans describe as 'one of the worst spot kicks imaginable'.

He was substituted by manager Lennie Lawrence and left the Kenilworth Road pitch in tears, his brief spell in this country over.

It had all started brightly for Bacque. He arrived on trial from Monaco, blond locks flowing. When he scored in friendlies against Arsenal and Coventry he looked as if he could be a real golden boy for Luton.

Bacque was given a year's contract and lined up for the first two league games of the new season. But after failing to score in either he would never make another league start.

Bacque was given a short-term deal at Motherwell but made just one appearance from the bench before moving to Norway. He was the golden boy who never quite managed to shine.

MACCLESFIELD TOWN

ANDREJUS TERESKINAS

Andrejus Tereskinas played 55 times for his country Lithuania before joining Macclesfield Town. He would play 54 games fewer for the Silkmen.

It looked to be the most unlikely transfer of the year when Peter Davenport announced he was signing the defender on a long-term loan from Skonto Riga. And so it proved. After eventually agreeing personal terms, Tereskinas was set to make his English debut in November.

'He has looked good in training' enthused his manager. It's the only time he ever did look good according to Macclesfield fans.

Injury followed injury. Work permit problem followed work permit problem. Postponed debut followed postponed debut. Eventually in February the great day finally arrived.

The man who had played Champions League football earlier that season lined up against Hartlepool – on the bench.

When he finally came on fans described him as looking confused. After the game, his mind cleared quickly and he was on the next plane back to Lithuania, his Macclesfield days – or rather day – over.

MANSFIELD TOWN

JOHNNY WALKER

In most places mention Johnny Walker and people think of a radio disc jockey or fine Scottish whisky.

But in Mansfield the name brings back memories of a diminutive Glaswegian midfield player. He stood just 5 feet 6 inches tall and weighed 10 stone – possibly not ideal for the rigours of England's lower leagues.

He was brought to England from Clydebank by the Grimsby manager Brian Laws. But almost all his spell at Clydebank had been spent in the reserves.

It was a different story at Field Mill where Walker played 36 times. He managed just three goals – one of those from the penalty spot – and lost his place near the end of the season.

He didn't get another chance until January the following season, but his substitute appearance against Hull turned out to be his last for Mansfield.

Johnny Walker headed back to his native Scotland. He had not been a big hit in England.

Detzi Kruszynski

MILTON KEYNES

DETZI KRUSZYNSKI

Wimbledon's signing of Detzi Kruszynski in 1988 wasn't so much a case of mistaken identity, more of mistaken geography. Or so his unimpressed colleagues would have you believe.

Bobby Gould signed Detzi in 1988. Legend has it, the manager believed he played for Hamburg rather than Homburg.

In fairness, Homburg – population 46,000; seating capacity at their Waldstadion ground 1,800 – were having the best spell in their history and briefly did appear in the Bundesliga before sliding back down the German leagues. But they could hardly be compared with Hamburg who twice won the German title in the 1980s and were a considerable force in Europe too.

The Polish under 21 international was never a regular for the Dons but was in and out of the side for three seasons and scored a handful of goals, before brief, unsuccessful spells at Brentford and Coventry.

He went on to coach children in the United States – where they didn't care whether he was a Homburger or a Hamburger!

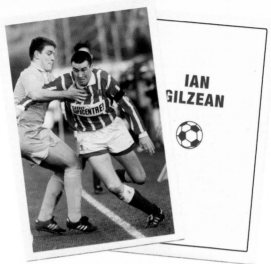

IAN
GILZEAN

NORTHAMPTON TOWN

IAN GILZEAN

The Golden Gilzeans are internet awards for ineptitude, stupidity and inadequacy at Northampton Town football club. Anybody who has shot themselves or the club in the foot is eligible. They are named after Ian Gilzean, the son of the famous former Spurs striker, Alan.

Gilzean was only at Northampton for one season, but it was the worst in the club's history. Scunthorpe scored seven goals against them and Rochdale six as they finished bottom of division three and lost their place in the Football League. To add to their misery, they were humiliated at home to non-league Bromsgrove Rovers in the first round of the FA Cup.

The Scot was actually the club's top scorer that season with 10 goals, but is still held responsible for their demise by many Cobblers' fans.

Gilzean was given a free transfer and played for clubs in Ireland and Scotland, before an injury sustained while playing for Montrose during the 2002–3 season ended his career.

NOTTS COUNTY

MIKAEL ANTOINE-CURIER

Mikael Antoine-Curier never puts down fitted carpets at home.

The restless soul made 29 appearances in the 2003–4 season – but for six different clubs.

His stay at Notts County was brief and controversial. The Frenchman joined the second division club on the 19th of February and left on the 19th of March after an alleged breach of club discipline. He had celebrated one goal and, tellingly, one birthday while he was there.

The next day he made his debut for Grimsby.

His stay at Meadow Lane was by no means his briefest of the season. The striker had left Oldham on the morning of September the 19th, 2003, joined Kidderminster Harriers that afternoon, played for 27 minutes against Rochdale the next day and left on the 22nd to join Rochdale and then Sheffield Wednesday.

Aged just 21, Mikael has already played for nine different English clubs. He's a young man in a hurry, but in danger of going nowhere fast.

OLDHAM ATHLETIC

NEIL MOORE

In the eyes of Oldham Athletic fans, Neil Moore was no Bobby Moore.

Moore was an old-fashioned stopper whose main strength was in the air. Yet Oldham fans remember his brief spell there harshly. One claimed he was so bad that it was hard to tell which team he was playing for. This was based on five games in a struggling side in 1994 during which time Oldham leaked nine goals.

Moore had spells at Norwich, Burnley and Macclesfield before drifting into non-league football.

However, he was given another chance to play in the league by Mansfield Town. He started the 2002–3 season at the heart of a defence which somehow conceded 28 goals in the first eight games – ironically including six against Oldham.

In all Moore played 18 times until a 5–4 home defeat by Bristol City marked the end of his spell in league football.

OXFORD UNITED

WAYNE BIGGINS

Wayne Biggins will for ever be 'Bertie' to fans of Stoke City who remember him with affection. After all, he had helped them win the Autoglass Trophy against Stockport at Wembley in 1992.

The fans at Oxford United had different names for him.

Biggins arrived at the Manor Ground under a bit of a cloud. He had served a 42-day ban after being sent off by referee Paul Alcock in what turned out to be his last ever game for Stoke.

Biggins had enjoyed a terrific career that took him to both Manchester City and Celtic. But he was almost 34 by the time he joined Oxford and never managed to win over the fans. His unorthodox gait when running made him the butt of supporters' jibes. He lasted just six months during which time he failed to score from open play – two penalties were all he had managed.

He then moved to Wigan, where ironically he scored on his home debut.

PETERBOROUGH UNITED

DAVID PLEAT

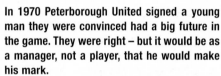

In 1970 Peterborough United signed a young man they were convinced had a big future in the game. They were right – but it would be as a manager, not a player, that he would make his mark.

David Pleat was a winger who, after a handful of games for Nottingham Forest, spent most of his career in the lower divisions with Luton, Shrewsbury and Exeter.

His move to Posh would be the beginning of the end for him. He played just one season and scored only twice.

From there Pleat drifted into non-league football with Nuneaton Borough, but was forced to retire from football with a bad back. Of course he had several of those as a manager!

He did, though, get the chance to show he had lost none of his winger's pace when he famously raced onto the field after his Luton side saved themselves from relegation by winning at Manchester City on the last day of the season.

PORT VALE

TOMMY WIDDRINGTON

The award-winning Tommy Widdrington was still playing for Macclesfield in the 2003–4 season 13 years after making his league debut. It's not certain if he remembers the reason for his award during his time at Port Vale, but Paul Furlong certainly will.

Only 90 seconds of Vale's game against Birmingham City had elapsed when Widdrington was red carded for drop-kicking Furlong. It was later judged to be the 'Most Psychotic Foul' of the season.

Off the field Tommy was mild-mannered – and hopefully still will be once he has read this – but on it, the red mist would often descend.

Crunching tackles, eye-balling and regular fights feature prominently on his CV during more than 300 league appearances. Tommy even managed to knock out the referee during a game for Hartlepool against Darlington – but this time he couldn't be blamed as the official had been pole-axed by a Widdrington blockbuster!

MATT DICKENS

ROCHDALE

MATT DICKENS

Matt Dickens only played four league games for Rochdale, but left a lasting impression – sadly not a good one.

The keeper was signed on a month's loan from Blackburn where, not surprisingly, with Tim Flowers, Bobby Mimms and Shay Given on their books he was struggling to get a game. He arrived at Spotland with a reputation for being 'a safe pair of hands'. Unfortunately, this didn't prove to be the case. By half-time on his debut at Wigan they were 4–0 down! The second half was goalless – the only 45 minutes during his stay when he didn't have to pick the ball out of the net. Four goals were put past him by Torquay in the next game, then three by Mansfield and another four by Carlisle. Poor Dickens had conceded 15 goals in four matches before returning shell-shocked to Ewood Park.

Later that season he went to Stockport where again he conceded four goals on his debut.

RUSHDEN & DIAMONDS

MICHAEL MISON

When Rushden & Diamonds needed goals most, they called on a man who had almost forgotten how to score. In the 1999–2000 season Rushden needed to beat Kidderminster in what was a Conference title decider. The winners would also clinch a Football League place.

In his hour-and-a-half of need, manager Brian Talbot called on Michael Mison to play up front. This was a surprise. Mison was a midfield player who had often borne the brunt of the crowd's criticism. It was more surprising still considering he had managed precisely two goals in two seasons and hadn't played for six months.

If Rushden had won Talbot would have been a genius and Mison a hero.

They lost 2–0 and finished second to Harriers.

Twelve months later they won promotion, but there was no happy ending for the stand-in striker. Mison never played for the club again, becoming an estate agent and joining non-league St Albans. Unfortunately his new employers wouldn't give him Saturday afternoons off, bringing a premature end to his career.

SCUNTHORPE UNITED

IAN BOTHAM

It is not often that struggling sides get the chance to sign an international superstar to beef up the team. But that's what happened to Scunthorpe United, a fourth division side, in 1980.

Botham, a strapping 24-year-old local lad, made his footballing debut as a substitute at Bournemouth in a 3–3 draw in March. He was on the bench in the next match before the new cricket season stumped him. It would be two years before he returned – in a 7–2 home defeat by Wigan. It wasn't until December 1983 – three-and-a-half years after the first of his infrequent appearances – that he was on the winning side, against Gillingham.

In all, he played 11 times. It's fair to say his mind may not always have been on football. It certainly wasn't during the famous Headingley test against the Australians in 1981 where he scored a marvellous unbeaten match-winning 149.

Sadly, he didn't score at all for Scunthorpe, let alone any match-winners.

SHEFFIELD WEDNESDAY

KLAS INGESSON

Sheffield Wednesday have been hurt more than most by expensive foreign flops over the years. The likes of Gilles de Bildes, Patrick Blondeau and Wim Jonk spring readily to mind, all picking up, rather than earning, huge pay packets. But perhaps the most disappointing of all was the giant Swede Klas Ingesson, signed from PSV Eindhoven.

He was no ordinary winger. At 6 feet 3 inches and more than 14 stone when he started a run at Hillsborough you could feel the tremors at Bramall Lane.

The trouble was the earth didn't move often enough. After his debut in August 1994, he didn't play again until December. The Swedish international managed just nine starts in his first season and three the next, before being packed off to Italy.

Ingesson was once deliciously described in the *Guardian* as 'a steam-powered version of Peter Crouch'.

His strike rate was similar as well – Ingesson scored just two goals in the Premiership. Mind you, he thumped them!

SHREWSBURY TOWN

VICTOR KASULE

Shrewsbury Town knew what they were getting when they paid £35,000 for the Glaswegian-Ugandan, Victor Kasule, in 1987.

In his time playing for Albion Rovers in Scotland, he was described as 'talented, but ludicrously ill-disciplined'.

It wasn't his talent that qualifies him for this book, it was his talent for getting into trouble.

He famously wrote off team-mate John Mcginlay's brand-new sports car, allegedly on an urgent trip to a local off-licence. On another occasion he was yellow carded for singing a George Benson song to the referee – it would have been red if it had been Lionel Ritchie!

Kasule was loaned to Darlington. He played just twice – but in his time there he managed to fall head-first out of a hotel window and dislocated a toe while acrobatically celebrating a goal.

He played 40 times in a couple of particularly eventful seasons at Gay Meadow, before the club realised there could be no taming of this Shrew.

He went back to Scotland to play for Hamilton where fans playfully dubbed him 'Vodka Vic'.

SOUTHEND UNITED

JEROEN BOERE

Southend fans loved to hate Dutchman Jeroen Boere. The former Go Ahead Eagles, West Ham and Crystal Palace player drove fans to phone BBC Radio's *6-0-6* calling him 'the laziest player ever to play for Southend United' as they were relegated to the second division in 1997. The striker signed by manager Ronnie Whelan was their top goalscorer – but had failed to reach double figures for the season.

If the supporters didn't like Boere, the feeling was mutual. He reportedly gave travelling supporters the 'V' sign during a game at Bournemouth, and the damage was irreparable.

Boere was top scorer again for the Shrimpers the following season, but his goals failed to win the fans over and no tears were shed at Roots Hall when he moved to Japan.

His story though has a tragic postscript. Boere lost his eye after being involved in a stabbing outside a bar in Tokyo and never played again.

STOCKPORT COUNTY

CARLTON PALMER

Even his best friends couldn't resist having a dig at Carlton Palmer. Ron Atkinson, who signed him twice, famously said 'Carlton can trap a ball further than I can kick it!'.

Despite his 18 England caps, Palmer has always been the butt of footballing jokes.

His time at his final club, Stockport County, where he was appointed player-manager in November 2001, started well enough. He scored in his first game as his team won their first home game of the season. But they lost their next 10 games and were relegated to the second division.

Things weren't much better in the next season. Of the 22 matches he started, Stockport won just eight. In the last of those matches in February, Palmer was sent off against Cheltenham, effectively ending his playing career – the sack from his manager's job soon followed.

He did turn up at Darlington later in the year but scored an own goal on his debut for the reserves putting any thoughts of a comeback on hold.

SWANSEA CITY

WALTER BOYD

Reggae Boy Walter Boyd set a world record during his stay at Swansea that will never be broken. The controversial Jamaican was sent off in zero seconds! Beat that!

Boyd, who had played for his country in the 1998 World Cup finals in France, arrived in Wales in October 1999. His reputation – already chequered after several red cards in Jamaica – hit rock bottom in a game at the Vetch Field against Darlington just six weeks later.

Coming on as a late substitute, play hadn't restarted before Boyd punched Darlington's Martin Gray and was immediately red carded by referee Clive Wilkes. The Swansea striker had been on the pitch for 57 seconds, but the ball had not been in play for any of that time.

Despite the incident John Hollins kept faith with Boyd who stayed at Swansea for two seasons. Not necessarily a bad player, but a very bad boy!

SWINDON TOWN

JASON DRYSDALE

It would be very brave or very foolish to suggest Neil 'Razor' Ruddock was Swindon's worst-ever player. Nevertheless it's fair to say he didn't fit in. Specifically, he didn't fit into his shorts. Ruddock was reported to have tried on all 90 pairs at the club, but kit suppliers eventually had to provide a specially made batch. On the field, Ruddock could play, and proved it with a scorching match-winner on his debut against Colchester.

Instead, most Swindon fans nominate former Watford and Newcastle full-back Jason Drysdale.

Drysdale was bought for £340,000 to replace the popular veteran Paul Bodin. He did – but only for the first game of the 1995–6 season before Bodin reclaimed his spot.

In three seasons Drysdale failed to establish himself as a first-team regular. Fans cruelly claim that he was more of a danger to the Swindon goal than opposition strikers were.

Even though he was only 28, Drysdale's days at the top were over as he moved to Forest Green Rovers and, from there, drifted down the leagues.

TORQUAY UNITED

DEAN MOONEY

With his bleached blond hair Dean Mooney looked more like a surfer than a soccer player. On the pitch, Torquay fans felt he was often all at sea too.

Mooney joined United in 1984 from Southern League side RS Southampton. The striker, who had scored a handful of goals for Leyton Orient and Bournemouth several years earlier, started the first seven games of the 1984–5 season. Torquay failed to score in most of them, Mooney in any of them, and he was dropped from the team.

When he got back into the team, he did manage goals against Wrexham and Halifax – but Torquay finished bottom of the Football League and had to apply for re-election for only the second time in their history.

Of the paltry 38 goals Torquay had scored, Mooney had contributed just two and was given a free transfer. It was back to the drawing board – or possibly, the surfboard.

DEAN MOONEY

TRANMERE ROVERS

GRAHAM BRANCH

So many players were almost Tranmere Rovers' worst-ever. Stand-up comedian Stan Boardman, BBC TV presenter Ray Stubbs and Chester Jets basketball coach Robbie Peers have all been on the books at Prenton Park. The problem is none of them was good enough even to get a first-team game.

Graham Branch started more than 100 league matches for Rovers after joining from the local amateur club Heswall in 1991. Described as a 'jet-paced winger' there was nothing jet-paced about his strike rate. In fact, he didn't score his first goal for the club until 1996, nearly five years after he first joined. It was his 32nd appearance.

Branch's goal-scoring did improve, but not a lot. The following season he would manage five goals – it was his most prolific time for the club. In seven stop-start seasons, Branch totalled just 10 goals, before moving on to carve out a successful career with Stockport and Burnley. But at Tranmere they remember him as oh-so-fast and oh-so-frustrating.

WALSALL

DALE BANTON

One man's hero is another man's villain – or so it seems. Almost every Walsall poll for their worst-ever player or worst-ever team includes one man – striker Dale Banton. It almost seems to go without saying.

True, he had a brief unsuccessful six months at the club in the 1988–9 season, but it seems harsh that he can be deemed the poorest-ever Saddler after such a short stint. Occasionally a Walsall fan will offer Bica, a Brazilian who managed 14 minutes of first-team action, as an alternative, but generally it's no contest.

Admittedly Banton failed to score in any of his 10 games for the club before moving on to Grimsby and finally back to Aldershot, where he fared little better.

Yet early in his career he had been so successful in his first spell at Aldershot that he attracted the attention of Millwall manager George Graham. He probably would have gone there, but the fourth division side wanted twice as much as Graham was willing to pay. Instead he went to York City, where his 49 goals puts him in some of their best-ever sides.

Loved at York, loathed at Walsall – that's Dale Banton.

MARK CARTWRIGHT

WREXHAM

MARK CARTWRIGHT

When things aren't going well the goalkeeper is often an easy target. At Wrexham in the 1998–9 season Mark Cartwright was that easy – and a big – target.

The 6 feet 2 inches tall keeper was being blamed by sections of the crowd for Wrexham's defensive failings, and club fanzines were awash with letters complaining that he wasn't up to scratch.

The fact that he was trying to replace the popular Andy Marriott, who had been sold to Sunderland, didn't help either. Nor did his defenders, who managed to score five own goals in a single season. After 30 consecutive games, the fans got what they wanted. Cartwright was dropped and never played for Wrexham again.

It wasn't the last we saw of him. After a brief spell at Brighton, he joined Shrewsbury Town. There was no happy ending there though. Cartwright played in their last two matches of the season – they lost them both and were relegated from the Football League.

WYCOMBE WANDERERS

STEWART CASTLEDINE

It was 'hello' and 'goodbye' in the same season for part-time model Stewart Castledine at Wycombe Wanderers. The former Wimbledon player had been a hero at Adams Park in the 1995–6 season when he produced a string of tremendous displays during a loan spell.

It was inevitable that when he returned on a permanent basis in 2000, he would be ring-rusty after just one game in two seasons for Wimbledon. But he managed just 17 league appearances – and started only six of those.

The only time he hit the headlines during his second spell was when his marriage to Lucy Alexander – Tamzin Outhwaite was a bridesmaid – was splashed on the front cover of celebrity magazine *Hello*. He was released at the end of the season and the same fans who had loved him, voted him Wycombe's worst-ever player in a recent poll.

Now Castledine does what those of us who could never play the game do – he presents TV programmes!

YEOVIL TOWN

ANDY TURNER

At 17 Andy Turner had the world at his feet. He had already made his Premiership debut for Spurs and after winning seven caps for the under 21s was thought to be a sure-fire future England star.

At 26 he was playing in the Conference with Yeovil as his form nosedived spectacularly.

When former Latvia manager Gary Johnson took over at Huish Park, he made Turner one of his first signings, hoping to find the key to reviving a flagging career. But Turner scored just once, against Hayes, before he was loaned out to Nuneaton. After a single season, the man once thought good enough to represent his country wasn't even thought to be good enough to play in the Conference and was released.

One man still had faith. Terry Fenwick, a former team-mate at Spurs, had signed Turner when he was manager at both Portsmouth and Crystal Palace. When Fenwick was made Northampton boss, he signed Turner again.

Fifteen days after the manager was sacked, so was Turner, after just 54 minutes in a Cobblers shirt.

ENGLAND'S WORST INTERNATIONAL

From the pinnacle of a playing career…

…it's a long way down

ENGLAND

ANDY GRAY

So you thought that David Beckham was rotten during England's ill-fated Euro 2004 campaign?

Thirteen years earlier England were struggling even to reach the Euro 92 finals in Sweden, so Graham Taylor took one of the gambles of his career.

Even though defeat in Poland could mean failure to qualify, Taylor axed his 90-cap skipper Bryan Robson, as well as Chris Waddle and David Batty.

Their places in the team went to Geoff Thomas, Andy Sinton and the uncapped midfielder Andy Gray.

At 27, the Crystal Palace player had rarely been in contention for an international spot. Now he was being asked to replace the legendary 'Captain Marvel' in a critical game. With Poland needing to win to reach the finals themselves, the atmosphere in the industrial city of Poznan was red-hot – too hot for the not-so-young debutant.

The game passed Gray by and at half-time, with Poland a goal up, he was substituted and replaced by Alan Smith. England survived thanks to a late Gary Lineker equaliser, but neither Gray nor Bryan Robson would ever play for England again.

Gray moved to Spurs in February 1992, but he was destined to struggle throughout his career. By Christmas he had been loaned to Swindon, and after a spell in Spain he eventually joined the Scottish side Falkirk.

There are of course many other contenders for England's worst-ever. Bolton's Michael Ricketts was another 45-minute flop when making his debut in Holland – it left him so traumatised that he didn't score again all season and was sold. Liverpool disregarded striker Paul Stewart's three goalless international appearances in 1992 and paid £2.3 million for him. Thirty-two club matches and one goal later, they wished they hadn't.

After his move from unfashionable Coventry to fashionable Arsenal, Jeff Blockley was capped in 1973 against Yugoslavia. When Roy McFarland was fit again, Blockley was swiftly out-of-fashion again. At least his solitary appearance puts him in good company. Colin Harvey, Charlie George, John Hollins, Steve Perryman, Brian Little and Tommy Smith are all also one-cap wonders!

INDEX

Acknowledgments
Thanks to David Todd, who supplied me with statistics and coffee in equal measure; Sky Sports; SEM; Jeff Weston; and Lizzie, Robbie, Matthew and Olivia for their patience and smiles.

First published in the United Kingdom in 2004 by
Weidenfeld & Nicolson
Wellington House, 125 Strand
London, WC2R 0BB

Text copyright © Jeff Stelling 2004

A CIP catalogue record for this book is available from the British Library

ISBN 0-297-84801-1

Printed and bound in Italy

Project Direction by Matt Lowing
Designed by D.R.Ink   info@d-r-ink.com
Picture Research by Katie Anderson
Index by Mike Solomons

The publishers would like to thank the following for permission to reproduce this material. Every care has been taken to trace the copyright holders. However, if there are any omissions we will happily rectify them in future editions.

Action Images: 2, 10, 12, 20, 32, 34, 38, 36, 69, 70, 74, 72, 76, 80, 84, 92, 96, 100, 104, 112, 113, 118, 119, 120, 124, 130, 131, 132, 133, 138, 142, 142, 143, 144, 145, 130, 148; Colorsport: 6, 8, 12, 16, 21, 24, 28, 30, 34, 48, 56, 60, 91, 109, 135, 138, 139, 140, 144; Empics: 16, 50, 54, 64, 66, 86, 88, 90, 94, 106, 108, 110, 111, 112, 113, 114, 116, 117, 118, 122, 123, 126, 128, 129, 130, 134, 136, 146, 147, 150, 151; *Sporting Pictures*: 16, 22, 56, 82, 107. Getty Images: 14, 26, 36, 40, 58, 64, 66, 68, 70, 96; Well Offside Images: 160; *Blackpool Gazette*: 105; *This is York*: 148; *Solent News* and Photo Agency: 46; Harold Finch: 62; Plymouth FC: 78; *Wigan Evening Post*: 98; *Hartlepool Mail*: 121; Mark Wilbraham, *Rochdale Programme*: 137.

Think you can do better? Send us your nomimations for football's worst.
worstfootballers@orionbooks.co.uk